REVOLT IN THE BLACK

Using the tax code to revolt against systematic oppression

Ricky Hinds

INTENTIONAL MEDIA

INTENTIONAL MEDIA
Intentional Media LLC
5510 Lincoln Street
Hollywood, Florida 33021

To Nia Brown-Hinds

You are proof that magic is real

CONTENTS

I am not a CPA, although this book has been reviewed by numerous CPAs for accuracy and technicality. **This book is in no way offering legal or professional advice and is intended to open your mind to the possibilities of using taxes as a tool to fund your growth and the growth of your community.** You should have any tax decisions reviewed by a CPA.

Prologue

When I was younger I wanted to free myself from the limited and isolated world of South Florida. Little did I know that as I got older and migrated further north and settled with my wife in Chicago, I would experience a world more limited than I ever imagined. Seeing the levels of segregation in Chicago and its surrounding neighborhoods has been an awakening experience. The joy of growing up black in south Florida is that you have the opportunity to experience so many different black cultures and people in one place. Needless to say, I am a black person that loves being around my people.

The more I traveled across this great planet, I began to see a pattern of underrepresentation of black and brown people in areas that are the "most desirable" within cities. The causes of underrepresentation are probably as unique to each country and continent as the Black people who live there. But the general trend implies systematic oppression, which should be alarming. However, the lack of black people in these places is treated as an expectation. This lack of black culture in many of the "must see" places around the world can be isolating when traveling. My amazing wife and I are currently traveling the world in hopes to bring black culture into the mainstream of tourism.

I wrote this book at a time when my wife and I were unsatisfied with the life we had created. She had passed the Illinois Bar exam and started working in education policy for Chicago Public Schools. After years of trying to create a successful tech startup, I landed what I believed to be a dream job with a high tech start up poised to change the world. We owned a condo in a trendy gentrifying neighborhood. By standard measures we had accomplished the American dream. But it felt as though we both bought into dreams that were not our own.

We devised an exit strategy, deciding to travel the world and chase our vision of happiness at all costs. In the planning for this great escape, I finally saw the US Tax Code for what our government intended it to be: a stimulus for invention and hedge against risk.

After leaving the start up and acquiring a remote work contract position, I reflected on my time at the start-up. I received a decent amount of stock options that bought my commitment to the company's dream. After about five months of becoming more active in Chicago's startup and development communities, I noticed a trend - there was a serious lack of black and brown people. Sure the company had "minorities." However, amongst those diversity numbers the majority were Asian. There were no Latinos, two black men and no black women. As a result there was a white culture that had never been exposed to black people. The results were frustratingly consistent displays of cultural appropriation and microaggressions. It was as though I was living a Dave Chappelle skit trying to avoid a "When Keeping it Real Goes Wrong" moment.

I attempted to help human resources by first making them aware of what microaggressions were. I then suggested some places to recruit more black people, and particularly black women. I even went as far as to suggest bringing in a highly qualified black female diversity consultant to work with the company, as well as the cooperative technology counsel to which they belonged. However, overtime it became clear that in the company's attempt to define a strategy for mass market profitability, they could not or would not focus on fixing their cultural issues.

In my attempts to help this young company, I was given a glimpse into how these large technology companies come to have such a lack of diversity. A small technology start up starts recruiting through a friends and family model. The first employees will typically look much like the founders of the company. Without a true human resources infrastructure, hiring continues to happen on a friend referral basis and thus the lack of diversity continues. Somewhere down the line perhaps a few minorities join the company in the late early stages, but at this point the snowball is too far down the hill. All the biases and cultural insensitivity from a homogeneous dominating culture are already set in place. People are not aware that there is a problem as they continue to search for candidates that "fit" the culture. As minorities trickle in slowly, they get further away from being one of the original members, and further away from significant amounts of ownership in comparison to the first groups of employees.

My experience at this start up opened my eyes to financial disparities due to the lack of business opportunities like working in a start up. I had spent the last two years prior to writing this book surrounded by black literature, black businesses, black art and social justice movements. My wife and I even instituted black movie Friday where we would only watch movies with a majority black cast. In all of this digestion of black culture I found myself frustrated with the seemingly endless systematic slights toward black people, but also fatigued with the studies and representations of the issues without any systematic methods of fighting back. This wary frustration led me a two part question. What do I believe is the greatest issue facing the black community and what system would I create to solve it? Answering this question has led me to create guidelines that could be reasonably followed towards a system of financial operations for our community.

I thank you for taking the time to read these words. I am humbled and encouraged by your interest. My intent is for this book to be a living document able to adapt to the people that it empowers.

Introduction

The beginning of a revolution doesn't have to hold the answers, it just needs to disrupt the establishment. Black and brown people in America are in the midst of fighting a 500 year war against European oppression. This book proposes that our freedom from oppression is intrinsically tied to our establishment of independent economic and community structures. More importantly, this book outlines how we can use existing business and tax law to create these structures.

Independent and self sustaining communities, like those established during Jamaica's inception, are key to survival and eventual thriving of black people in America. In my native Jamaica, the foundation for independence was an exemplary community that was financially, militarily, agriculturally and culturally independent of British colonizers established by the legendary Maroon Nanny. Some say Nanny was a slave that escaped with her brothers into the mountains; and other accounts insist Nanny was a royal Ashanti princess who sailed to Jamaica.[1]

---

[1] "Jamaica's True Queen: Nanny of the Maroons." Jamaicans.com, 2015, Jamaicans.com/queennanny. Accessed 9 December 2016.

Nanny and her brothers created villages in the Blue Mountains of Jamaica.[2] These villages were self sustaining communities that provided a haven for escaping slaves.[3] Nanny assumed the role of "chieftainess or wise woman" and passed down legends, customs, songs and music descendant from Africa.[4] These teachings were the basis of confidence and resolve in the Maroon warriors living there.[5] Nanny, famed for her leadership qualities and guerrilla warfare tactics, lead a rebellion in the first Maroon War, a battle between free Blacks and British soldiers .[6] Due to the cultural foundation of independence Nanny created, Jamaicans were able to fight slavery until the early 1800s when the British officially abolished slavery on the island.

---

[2] Craton, Michael. Testing the Chains. Cornell University Press, 1982, p. 89-90

[3] Ibid.

[4] "Nanny of the Maroons. Jamaican Information Service." 2017, http://jis.gov.jm/heroes/nanny-of-the-maroons/. Accessed 20 January, 2017.

[5] Ibid.

[6] Ibid.

Although Jamaicans began to partake in economic and political systems that were set up by the British colonials, we maintained our culture, adapted from the Ashanti, which eventually delivered independence. A nation run by the black people sent to work its lands.

I believe that revolutions are driven by two factors, social outrage and economics. In my opinion, we have been outraged about social injustice and have done a great job organizing and fighting for equality under the law. Outrage about economic inequality, while well documented, seems to have not gotten the organization it deserves. In this book, I attempt to offer some strategies to enable you to legally limit financial losses to taxation by creating businesses, thereby empowering yourself and your community by forcing the government to invest in YOU via your tax dollars.

Taxes Matter

Taxation (at a time when there was no income tax) was one of if not <u>the</u>, major cause of the American revolution.[7] Today income tax rates are around 10% to 35% .[8] Not to mention sales, and social security taxes.[9] I can see you saying to yourself - why do I care? After all as Benjamin Franklin famously said, "Nothing is certain except death and taxes".[10]

But you should understand that white families historically have had the ability to earn money and pass it on to their families with limited payment to the government, while we, people of color, essentially paid 100% taxes through slave labor and sharecropping respectively

---

[7] Permanent income taxes were not imposed until 1913 through ratification of the 16th amendment. History of the US Income Tax. The Library of Congress. https://www.loc.gov/rr/business/hottopic/irs_history.html. 2004. Accessed 24 January 2017." Parliamentary taxation of colonies, international trade and the American Revolution, 1763-1775" Office of the Historian. Department of State. https://history.state.gov/milestones/1750-1775/parliamentary-taxation. Accessed 24 January 2017.

[8] "2017 Tax Brackets." Tax Foundation. taxfoundation.org/article/2017-tax-brackets Retrieved 16 November 2016. Internal Revenue Service "2016 Federal Tax Rates, Personal Exemptions and Standard Deductions" Internal Revenue Service. https://www.irs.com/articles/2016-federal-tax-rates-personal-exemptions-and-standard-deductions. Accessed 24 January 2017. At the time this book was written we were living in a Pre-Trump Era - these rates are subject to change with his presidency.

[9] Ibid.

[10] Smyth, Albert Henry The Writings of Benjamin Franklin, Vol. X (1789-1790). New York: MacMillan. (1907). p. 69.

up until the 1950's or later depending on the state. This tax was not paid into government programs to benefit future generations; it was paid to white families that were free to partake in the economically discriminatory system. An economic system that saw to the United States become one of the world's wealthiest and financially powerful nations. These families have financially benefited exponentially on the interest free loan of our ancestors labor.

Now, many of those discriminatory legal restraints preventing African-American from full economic participation have been outlawed. Yet there has been no repayment acknowledging the hundreds of years of blatant economic discrimination. No systematically impactful financial contribution, such as free education or 300 years of tax free income for African-American families has been provided. We, as a people, must remember that we are only two generations removed from forced 100% taxation. I do not believe any black person in the western world should be required to pay taxes for 300 years, but this tax break will not be handed to us. We will need to take it.

The average black household income in 2014 was just above $35,000 .[11] Adjusting for inflation let's say today's average income is $40,000 a year. For the sake of this example, let's say you will make this throughout your lifetime. Assuming you have fifty working years, we'll compare the amount of money you would make at today's tax rate compared to the amount of money you would make without paying any taxes. Granted this example is inherently flawed due to the lack of adjustment for inflation, but the illustration will prove the point that in order to adequately "catch up" and achieve economic equality, we'll need to reduce the amount of taxes being paid by black people. Without taxes you would make $2 million vs $1.4 million over your lifetime. That is more than half a million dollars that could be used to provide investments for future family members. Over half a million dollars that could be used to pay for exceptional early childhood education to propel your children educationally and financially. This is also just half a million for one individual. Multiply this by the estimated 16.57 million black

---

[11] *Income and Poverty in the United States: 2014*. U.S. Department of Commerce Economics and Statistics Administration. U.S. CENSUS BUREAU. Table A-1 p 26. http://www.census.gov/content/dam/Census/library/publications/2015/demo/p60-252.pdf

households as of 2015, based on black Americans being 13.3% of the population ,[12] you begin to see how impactful this taxed income could be.

The issue of paying taxes in the United States has become a moral dilemma. As the radical presidential candidate Donald Trump brags about not paying taxes for years, we demonize his use of the tax code because he is not paying his fair share. Yet, Donald Trump has simply used the resources available to him by our economic system. The same resources available to all of us. From my own observation, it seems as though many people do not take advantage of tax loopholes because there is a lack of education on the subject and a general fear surrounding the use of these loopholes.[13] I believe the key to a black economic revitalization is the aggressive and systematic exploitation of these perfectly legal tax deductions.

---

[12] "Quick Facts" United States Census Bureau. census.gov/quickfacts/table/RHI125215/00 Retrieved 18 November 2016

[13] " 5 Things Taxpayers Are Irrationally Afraid Of - And Shouldn't Be." Kelly Phillips Erb. 12 April 2015. forbes.com/sites/kellyphillipserb/2015/04/12/5-things-taxpayers-are-irrationally-afraid-of-and-shouldnt-be/#706ab5a2225c. Accessed 12 April 2015.

Wealthy families know the greatest risk to their generational wealth is taxes. The government makes an attempt to return some of this stolen money that was gained through the advantages of segregation and discrimination. I say “stolen money” from my perspective as a black man, born in the western world, a descendant of sugar plantation slaves in the Caribbean.

The United States and other nations have implemented an estate tax, which means that anyone with a certain amount of money, today it's about 5.49 million dollars , will be taxed a percentage as high as 40% upon their death.[14] Theoretically the stolen money would go back to the government for wealth redistribution into resources for all Americans, which should eventually even the playing field over time.

The problem with the estate tax is the government has an inability to collect this money in many cases because the concept of ownership allows for creativity when it comes to taxes. For example, if you create a trust you can place your property, anything of value from a busi-

---

[14] “Estate Tax” Internal Revenue Service. 28 October 2016. irs.gov/businesses/small-businesses-self-employed/estate-tax Last Accessed 16 November 2016.

ness to real property, under the control of the trust relinquishing your ownership rights. So when you die, you are taxed nothing and those who you've given access to the trust can access all of the resources you've stored within it. What is a trust? Is it a person or a place? No it is just bunch of papers filed with the government establishing a relationship that holds property on behalf of a beneficiary. The trust, or relationship, is not a person or property and thus cannot be taxed even though it has property rights. Sure, assets might be taxed when they are placed in the trust; but those with enough foresight know to place these assets in the trust when they are lower in value. This means the assets will grow tax free for the beneficiaries. I believe that these concepts of ownership, as abstract and perverse as the ownership of human bodies, elude the core strategies and identities of our black community.

Someone once told me that some Native Americans believed that European greed was a sickness when they first encountered them. Some Anishinaabe (Native Americans from northern US & Canada) believed early Europeans to suffer from"*wétigo*" or "soul sickness" which caused them to "consume the souls of other people with their greed."[15] They believed this based on the European need for exclusive ownership and their inability to share or concern for future generations.[16] How it is someone could believe they have the right to own a mountain, let alone people? Yet this concept of ownership has infected us all. But if the world is already sick or infected, we need to at least understand the thing that plagues us.

We face systematic genocide in America that would have been met with bloody and violent revolution in a time when riffles were the height of military technology. I believe there is a place for violence when faced with opposition that desires nothing but your extinction. But a system cannot be fought simply with violence, it must be opposed by an equivalent systematic approach. We can and must take the systems of the oppressor and use it to build our community.

What You Will Get Out of This Book

---

[15] "Indian 201: Soul Sickness." Ojibwa. 18 October 2011. http://www.dailykos.com/story/2011/10/18/1027504/- Accessed 1 December 2016.

[16] Ibid.

- Understanding of your rights to establish yourself as a business and take financial risks.
- How to organize your lifestyle around your business to maximize tax deductible business expenses.
- How to use your tax return to pivot your business.
- Strategies for financial community organizing to resolve issues within the black community.

Chapter 1

Business vs Employee

Employees Forfeit Their Rights

As an Independent contractor you are paid without having taxes withheld. It is your responsibility to pay your taxes at the end of the year. The company that paid you is responsible for recording this payment on their taxes and providing you with a 1099. You will then have a clear paper trail of income that you will be required to report.

This delayed taxation might seem like an inconvenience, but you are simply being treated like a business. Like Fortune 500 companies that employ many people and deduct the costs associated with their operations, as an independent contractor you are given the liberties of business expenses. Let's say you cut lawns for a living and you are paid as an independent contractor. You could deduct gas and maintenance for the lawn mower, any expenses in traveling to the job site, so long as it is considered a temporary work location, and any relevant education classes you believe you need to grow your business. This could include landscaping classes, business classes and possibly some electronic engineering classes. The more expenses you accumulate in an effort to grow your business, which in many cases means investing in yourself, the less you will need to pay in taxes for the money you make.

Adversely, as an employee of a lawn service company you've essentially given up your right to be considered a business. This is because it is presumed your employer will determine what are relevant business expenses to grow their business. As an employee you are simply a part of business operation expenses. This means the company determines what expenses will be paid for by the company, which may not include investing in your education or commute.

In this example there is no difference in your job function. You are going out and cutting lawns for a living. In one situation you are employed and in another you are doing it as an independent contractor. With the filing of a W2 form you lost your right to be a business for that particular work. I'm not telling you to never become an employee. I simply wish to demonstrate to you how legal forms change your rights and tax eligibilities. This book will show you how to use the tax benefits of being a business in combination with employment to return the tax withheld from your day job income.

Governments respect business, not people

The United States operates based on a mixed economic system, blending aspects of socialism but driven by businesses. You could characterize the founding of the United States itself as a business expansion of the British crown. Early european settlers were able to build trading industries so long as they paid taxes to the British empire. Today, large corporations collude to impact the laws which affect our lives. For example, an organization named American Legislative Exchange Council (ALEC) creates boilerplate drafts of potential laws and policies that enable state legislator to simply add their state and sign their names to propose legislation.[17] ALEC is funded by some of the United States largest companies. To get a good look at the companies involved in ALEC and the thousands of laws being written by the organization take a look at alecexposed.org. It may feel as though your elected officials are sometimes working against your best interest and often times, in my opinion, this is because they are working for corporations.

This is not an indictment of the political and financial structure of the country. Before we completely vilify our elected officials we must examine both the pur-

---

[17]"Further Reading, "Oops: Florida Republican Forgets To Remove ALEC Mission Statement From Boilerplate Anti-Tax Bill." Alex Seitz-Wald. Think Progress. thinkprogress.org/oops-florida-republican-forgets-to-remove-alec-mission-statement-from-boilerplate-anti-tax-bill-f595c95a844#.y3leb7t76

pose of for-profit organizations and the foundational purpose of the United States.

We must understand financial and political structures if we are going to be able to use or duplicate them. Shareholders are the individuals or entities that have purchased a percentage of the company, therefore owning part of the company. For profit corporations exist to maximize shareholder value. Managers of these for profit organizations have a legal obligation to maximize shareholder value. Shareholder value can be interpreted in many ways. Typically stock price, the price it costs to buy a single share that represents fractions of percentage of ownership, determine the value of shareholder ownership. These stock prices are heavily influenced by profits .[18] This single minded purpose of profit is at the foundation of every for-profit organization. Some altruistic companies have been able to take a long term and liberal approach to what is valuable for shareholders, such as weighing the environmental or social effects of a decision and how it will affect the shareholders. Most com-

---

[18] "How Do Profits Reflect Stock Prices?" Terry Lane. Zacks Investment Research. finance.zacks.com/profits-reflect-stock-prices-8263.html Accessed 19 November 2016.

panies, however, seek to maximize profits ,[19] even if their actions adversely affect the country as a whole.

The United States exists to continue to exist, based on the belief that its union will serve the long term benefits of not only its citizens, but also the citizens of the world at large. The US sees being a world superpower as essential to its survival and democracy as a whole. Maintaining this level of relevance requires both military dominance and financial power. The second of these two factors drives government entanglement with businesses, resulting in legally instilled governmental respect for companies' liberties and needs over that of you, a lone citizen.

This truth goes against the American story, that our government exists, "Of the people, by the people, for the people..."[20] There is an inherent conflict in this prioritization of business because profit driven companies do not exist only for the good of the people. For example,

---

[19] "We Need To Stop Maximizing Profit And Start Maximizing Value." Henry Blodget. Business Insider. 8 December 2012. businessinsider.com/lets-stop-maximizing-profit-and-start-maximizing-value-2012-12 Accessed 19 November 2016.

[20] Lincoln, Abraham. "Gettysburg Address" Dedication of the Soldier's National Cemetery, Gettysburg.

members of ALEC commonly propose laws that have the potential to make the lives of everyday citizens worse in hopes of generating increased profits and provide more tax revenue for our government. The taxed income not only goes into supporting the financial power of the country, but should make the lives of citizens better through investment in social funded projects and programs such as schools and infrastructure development.

Logically the investment into businesses over people might make sense. Business entities like governments do not die, so long as they have financial resources and people continue to participate in running them. Businesses are more predictable. A business is less likely to squander the investment of government because it has a distinct purpose that supports the financial strength of the government. When a business chooses a location as its home base it can lift the finances of an entire city or, in rare cases, an state or countries like Samsung does for South Korea .[21] A business can unite many people under one identity. A single individual's potential

---

[21] "Could the Samsung Crisis Affect South Korea's National Economy?" Reuters. 18 October 2016. NBC NEWS. nbcnews.com/tech/tech-news/could-samsung-crisis-affect-south-korea-s-national-economy-n668081. Accessed 25 January 2017.

cannot be made up of many people. Also the purpose of that person can change on a whim.

How does a lone citizen hope to compete with multinational corporations for government respect and attention? Its simple really. If you can't beat them, join them. Don't be a lone citizen, become a business. This way when our communities gather to lend our suggestions on our governance, we are doing so as businesses of untold size an influence. These businesses will ransom the income tax revenue that the government depends on. Eventually our businesses will be able to lobby, organize and advocate under our own shadow organizations serving the distinct needs of our communities. Might I suggest **Colored American Legislative Exchange Council (CALEC).**

A world without W2 employment

Imagine a world where with no employees and instead everyone was an independent contractor. We would all determine the valid expenses relevant to self contained businesses. For most people the amount of taxes they pay would drop significantly as they deduct all manor of related education, travel, home offices, and equipment expenses. There would certainly be a number of people without the wherewithal to pay their taxes accurately and on time or who simply forget to pay taxes at all. For the independent contractor or business it would be ideal. For the IRS, it would be an absolute nightmare. The amount of labor needed to track down the masses not paying taxes would be extremely expensive. The number of audits would exponentially increase. The size of the government spending for the IRS would certainly increase. This is an important concept to grasp because the way we choose to provide labor, either through independent contracting or W2 employment, has a profound impact on the government's ability to efficiently collect taxes. W2 employment provides a way for the government to manage collecting and reporting of taxes in a society with an ever increasing population. The responsibility of reporting taxes are placed on large corporations allowing for the consolidation of thousands of individuals' tax reporting into one entity that is responsible for deciding what are valid business expenses.

Larger corporations are more stable in their year to year and even day to day business operations than individuals, making it easier over time for the IRS to handle auditing these companies. Without the consolidation of individual taxes, accurate and cost efficient collection would probably be impossible. However, this limitation of our government to collect taxes is not your problem. Nor do you have to conform to the convenient structure of W2 employment. To do so, is to forfeit your right of deducting valid businesses expenses in the business that is you.

Chapter 2

Become A Business

Just trying could save you a lot of money

To become a business you only need to file a bit of paperwork with your state government. In many cases you don't need to file any papers, but then the burden of proof is a bit harder when deal with the IRS if you are audited. Simply file articles of incorporation for your state of choice and then apply for a free EIN number on a government website. The EIN is not mandatory, but it makes your life easier when trying to do things that require federal documentation such as open a business bank account.

The beauty of an LLC is something called pass through taxation. This means you can deduct the net operating losses for your business from your overall taxes owed. Your overall taxes are calculated based on all your income, including income from your W2 employment aka your 9 to 5. As a result deductions for businesses expenses incurred by the LLC are passed through to your individual taxes and can thus reduce the amount of money owed in taxes.

To illustrate, let's say you worked a job as a W2 employee this year and had taxes deducted. During tax season you prepare your taxes and discover the government has overtaxed you by $1,000. This means you are entitled to $1,000 in tax return money. However, if you also operated a side business resulting in a net operating loss (income - expenses) of $10,000, you would also be eligible to receive that additional money on your tax return ($10,000 is not a qualifying number. It is just a random amount being used for this example. You could have net operating loss of more or less). This is because the net operating loss has reduced the amount of taxes owed by $10,000. So if you paid at least $11,000 in taxes that year, you would receive your $10,000 in deduction and the $1,000 that you overpaid back on your tax return.

This also means that income from your business also gets added to your individual taxes and can change your tax bracket resulting in owing more tax on your overall income. Using the same average black household income adjusted for inflation at $40,000 a year, as of 2016 you will pay 32.65% in taxes, not including whatever sales tax you end up paying. This means you will only net $26,940. Now you won't be able to get all of the taxes you pay back because you cannot deduct against Social Security and Medicare taxes, which account for 7.65%. However, pick the business appropriate for your lifestyle, and make spending decisions in line with that business, and you can get your $10,000 back, 25% income tax, from the IRS and maybe have some net operating losses to carry forward .[22] That's right, if you have more losses than the amount of money that you are being taxed, then you can carry the remainder over for years to come. This is how presidential candidate Donald Trump has supposedly not paid taxes for 20 years after losing a reported $916 million in expenses .[23]

Owning a business in the US has no requirement that you continue the same business plan from year to year. There is also no requirement that your business is

---

[22] "What You Should Know About Net Operating Loss Carryback Rules" Stephen Fisherman, J.D. Lawyers.com. http://taxation.lawyers.com/business-taxation/what-you-should-know-about-carryback-and-carryforward-rules.html. Accessed 25 January 2017.

[23] "How a Simple Tax Rule Let Donald Trump Turn a $916 Million Loss Into a Plus" Nicholas Confessore, Binyamin Appelbaum. New York Times. nytimes.com/2016/10/04/us/politics/donald-trump-taxes.html Accessed 20 November 2016.

limited in scope to one particular activity, unless you are in certain heavily regulated industries such as banking and financials. Again using our average black household income of $40,000. If you get your $10,000 from deducting net operating losses, you could change your business operations completely in the following year. You could stop your practice of being an online personality or writer for example and become a real estate investor. Heck you could do both simultaneously in some bizarre social media investing hybrid. No one can attempt to validate your idea or your pursuit of profits. The IRS typically gives you around three consecutive years of reporting net operating losses before they closely scrutinize your business deductions. However, so long as you are operating a real business then there is nothing to worry about.

On a macro level, what I would like to see is a $165 billion dollar a yearly stimulus package, not given to black communities, but generated by our own ingenuity as a result of turning the individual into a business. Just to expound on our previous example, let's take a macro view when looking at the average black households' income of $40,000. The total number of households in the

United States is approximately 124.6 million.[24] While the total percentage of black people in the United States (13.3%) does not equate to the percentage of black households, we can use total percentage of black people in the US as a decent estimate. We will say that 13.3% of the 124.6 million households are black households. This means there are approximately 16.57 million black households in the US. As a result black households approximately generated $662.872 billion of income when we take our $40,000 average black household income and multiply it by the 16.57 million black households . That gives us $165.71 billion of income tax, 25% of income taxed on the $662.872, that could be used to invest in our own communities.

Why would the IRS give anyone so much power to create a business based on anything? It's simply because they have no choice. The government cannot become a gatekeeper or approver for what constitutes a valid business. Innovation is the lifeblood of the world economy. Engineers and everyday people create all manner of gad-

---

[24] "Number of households in the U.S. from 1960 to 2015 (in millions)" https://www.statista.com/statistics/183635/number-of-households-in-the-us/ Accessed 20 October 2016.

gets, trinkets, and services that would seem absolutely pointless or hard to understand. Then all of a sudden the unheard of thing sells millions or billions of dollars worldwide adding to the US Gross Domestic Product (GDP).

Take for example something that I find absolutely ridiculous but brilliant, emoji's. Emoji's are simple icons. Digital images that can be sent with a message or as a message. The social bloom of emojis have made them a valid means of communication creating value for the symbols. Today there are many different emoji apps available for download. The creation and distribution of emojis is a major business industry in the digital world. Some reports even claim that emojis are the fastest growing language .[25] In fact, this year, 2016, comedian Kevin Hart released his own line of emojis selling for $1.99 on the apple marketplace.[26] The app also features the ability

---

[25] "UKs Fastest Growing Language is Emoji" Anna Doble. BBC. 19 May 2015. bbc.co.uk/newsbeat/article/32793732/uks-fastest-growing-language-is-emoji. Accessed 20 November 2016.

[26] "Kevin Hart Emoji App Leaps to No. 1 on Apple App Store Paid Chart" Todd Spangler. Variety. 14 September 2016. variety.-com/2016/digital/news/kevin-hart-emoji-app-apple-itunes-paid-chart-1201860741/. Accessed 20 November 2016.

to download additional emoji's for $0.99, providing an ever growing revenue stream. If left to a government bureaucrat to validate the business value of emojis we might not have our eggplants and side eyes.

Imagine what the world would look like if each business idea required validation from the IRS. You would need to apply for each new business idea. Maintaining and updating the laws as well as the forms themselves for the application process would require a host of new government employees. The review process would take years of denials and appeals just to start your business. The oversight of your organization's operations to ensure that you are within the strict guidelines provided for your business's existence would also require many new government employees. The process of this type of regulation would be so expensive that creating new industries would be an expense to our government.

The IRS has two important distinctions when it comes to business expenses. There are start up expenses and business operating expenses. Start up expenses refer to any expenses related to getting your business off the ground. This could include investigation expenses such as taking a trip somewhere for research, filing fees like those associated with your llc registration, or even buying a laptop. The problem with start up expenses is that you are limited to how much of this expense is deductible in a given year. You can deduct up to $5000 in the first year and then any additional expenses are broken evenly over 180 months .[27] So, if you had $20,000 as start up expenses, $5000 will be deducted from your current year's taxes and then $15,000 divided by 180 then multiplied by twelve will give you the amount you can deduct each year until the full remaining $15,000 is deducted. In this example you would deduct about $1000 over 15 years. Business operating expenses on the other hand, as presidential candidate Donald Trump has showed us, have no limitations on how much can be deducted in a given year. If you have expenses that are more than your income taxes then the remainder of the expenses will be rolled over to the next tax year.

Business operating expenses are expenses incurred while you are operating your business. The obvious question is, when does your business stop being in

---

[27] "Costs You Can Deduct or Capitalize" Internal Revenue Service. irs.gov/publications/p535/ch07.html#en_US_2015_publink1000208919 Accessed 20 November 2016.

the getting off the ground or start up phase and begin operations. The answer is anytime you want depending on what your business operation is. As a writer for example your business is to read, observe and write. This business operation can start immediately. The beauty of owning a business in the United States is that the government has limited ability to validate what is considered a business or business operations. Do not make the mistake of only reporting your business's expenses as start up expenses. Use both if you need to. Deduct anything you deem as a start up expense up to $5000, then start your business operations and count all your additional expenses as business operating expenses.

Ideas

Anything can be a business, so long as you believe someone will eventually pay for it, and it is legal under the law of your state. Your business can have multiple operations that are directly related, or completely independent. For instance, if you are a social media personality, but also do hair, and provide recipes online, all of that can be your business. The combination of these operations can give you a significant amount of deductible expenses. The goal of any idea is not just to make it look like you are running a business but to *actually* run a business. It will require some work on your part, but consider the money you will receive back from the IRS from your tax returns. Not to mention you might even start generating significant income.

The likelihood that someone will begin a business generating significant income on day one, especially the type of income that allows you to quit your day job, is unlikely. A more likely scenario is that you will make small amounts of income, but it will not outpace the paycheck from your day job. So if you do not have confidence in one particular profitable business plan, instead of focusing on one potential profit making idea, focus on numerous operational ideas. This will accomplish two things. First you will be able to quickly evaluate and try multiple means of making money, which could also lead to an interesting niche. The second thing testing out multiple business plans does is maximizing amount of business operations you have available. This increases the likelihood that the majority of your spending is encompassed of business operations, making the majority of your spending tax deductible.

Anything you create that you can sell becomes a business. What might seem to be a kids art project can be a business. Making beaded jewelry, home crafts, and random art projects can all be considered a business, so long as you are trying to achieve profitability through these activities. Just pop up a Squarespace, Shopify or Amazon account, start selling and wala instant business. Even if you sold your art projects on the street or door to door, this could be considered a business with business expenses. The key is to think about how to monetize the things that you are already doing.

As ridiculous as it might sound, your social media presence can be a business today. Social media is one of the most accessible opportunities for the average taxpayer to create a business. Social media has the potential to generate income and provide a wide range of tax deductibility for business expenses. Your moments in life are a valuable and entertaining product. Facebook, Twitter, Instagram, SnapChat and other social media platforms all package your moments, shared as pictures, videos and messages, to figure out the most efficient way to deliver them to viewers. This enables the social media companies to charge advertisers money to put ads on your screen while you are watching these moments. It's very similar to the way radio and television generate income, with the exception that those creating the entertainment are not getting paid a percentage of the billions the products create. By simply creating a blog and posting all your moments there you now have a business that can generate ad income and business expenses.

Linking your blog to social media outlets provides you a distribution channel for your product (your moments). Add advertising to your blog, which is easy with platforms like Squarespace, and your business is generating income immediately. The best part is you will probably be posting to social media anyway; but just by popping up your own blog and adding the advertising, you're hobby can become a business. Your social media now becomes promotional space for your business, your blog, where you can post teaser content.

To fully illustrate the potential benefits that a social media centered business can offer let's evaluate an addictive collectors item, Jordans. Personally, I don't understand sneakerhead culture and the obsession buying new and exclusive pairs of these shoes for WAY above the production cost.[28] However this hobby, highly criticized for its financial wastefulness, does create the opportunity for a valid social media business. Let's say your online presence is centered around your collection and evaluation of exclusive and expensive Jordans. By posting images and videos of these shoes online, or writing reviews of these items, you can justify their purchase as a business expense. This would make your purchase of Jordan's, which you probably would be purchasing anyway, a fully qualified business operating expense because it is essential to your social media business.

What makes adding a social media operation such a beneficial part of your income strategy for your business is that it touches so much of your life. Everything you display is a potential tax deduction. If there is a particular place in your home dedicated to taking selfies that area can be subtracted from the total square footage of your place as a tax deduction, so long as it is not being used for any other purpose. The clothes you buy particularly for the purposes of going out to take pictures. The

[28] "A Field Guide to the Modern Day Sneakerhead" Jian Deleon. Complex Magazine. 13 July 2015. http://www.complex.com/sneakers/sneakerhead-guide Accessed 6 December 2016.

events you go to. Even your gym membership may qualify as a deduction because your appearance and body may be essential to your social media personality. With the growing revenue from social media and almost endless iteration on social media features, the IRS' subjective approach to determining what is a business will need to be lenient to the rise of social media based businesses because predicting what will become popular, and thus financially valuable in the world of social media is impossible.

For those looking to get into the real estate investments, you don't need to be the next Donald Trump with a million dollar investment project. What you should be looking for are undervalued neighborhoods. The great part of being black is that we typically know more about some neighborhoods that are undervalued because they are our own communities. Think of the once illustrious appeal of Harlem for black opulence in New York City. Its fall to poverty, crime and obscurity, and its resurgence as it fights to maintain against gentrification. Within our neighborhoods we have a unique insight and opportunity for investment. It would be a declaration of fighting against oppression if we were able to purchase all the land and buildings within black communities.

Where there is an empty lot that seems to serve no purpose, turn it into a functioning community garden. As a community garden you can choose to operate it as a for-profit business, renting space for others to grow their products that can be sold at a self-organized farmers market. You could take a percentage of the proceeds from sale or charge a flat rental fee for farm space. Alternatively you could run the garden as a non-profit, providing food to the neighborhood at no cost. With both strategies you have the benefit of deducting the expenses associated with operating the business or nonprofit. In the case of the non-profit you will be charging the non-profit to rent the space that you own personally. You can either donate your personal income to pay the rent or collect donations to help pay the rent. Donating your money means you get to deduct the amount donated as a charitable gift donation from your personal income tax. No matter how you choose to manage your real estate, the property taxes you would typically have to pay, become a tax deductions as well as any maintenance, repairs, and improvements needed for operation. This is one of my favorite strategies because there is so much opportunity in urban cities, like Detroit, where there is an abundance of urban lots waiting to be reimagined.

When brainstorming a business idea, I suggest you focus on these three questions to start:

i. What do you spend your money on?

ii. How can I adjust my lifestyle to qualify my spending as a business expense?

iii. Do I need to adjust my spending habits to achieve significant qualified business expenses?

Remember, the initial goal is to start a business that allows you to get as much of your tax money back on your tax return so that it can then be used to invest in an income generating business or long term investment. Be brave, and remember it does not matter how many initially buy what it is that you are selling, success is never guaranteed with any business. Just trying can pay you with the taxed revenue from your day job.

Chapter 3

Achieving Maximum Tax Deductible Coverage

Letting your life work for your business

The first thing I want to make very clear and reiterate is that I am **NOT** telling you to create a shell business. This is where you put in no effort towards profitability and have a business in name only. This is illegal. The IRS requires you put significant time into your business. How much time is significant time? It's actually vague and undefined. A good rule of thumb and probably the minimum effort for running a micro business that anyone can achieve, is probably an average of 1 hour a day working on your business. Now again, what is considered work for your business is up to you. What matters is that you are seeking profitability. Keeping track of your business expenses and making sure that your spending aligns with your business activity means you will need to have business activity. This entire process will be a part time second job. You probably won't have to go into an office or to a job site, but creating the activity you'll need to achieve Maximum Tax Deductible Coverage will be work.

Maximum Tax Deductible Coverage is covering as much of your expenses as possible under business expenses. This is something you want to achieve every year you are running a business, but it is particularly important for those whose business is not their primary source of income. Achieving Maximum Tax Deductible Coverage results in generating investment money from your taxed primary income. You work a little harder, so you can get more net income from your current job, by passing business expenses through to your personal taxes.

Monthlyexpensecalcultor.com provides a useful list of common monthly expenses.[29] Using the information provided there, let's review some common monthly living expenses, explore potential deduction strategies, and gain an idea of the flexibility offered in the tax code. Specifically we will look at: rent/mortgage payments, utilities, auto loan/lease payments, maintenance and repairs, cell phone, internet, television, groceries, dining

---

[29]monthlyexpensecalculator.com provides a list of common monthly expenses to enable users to visualize a budget.

out, and vacation costs. That's a lot of expenses, but we'll go through each one. **Again, make sure you read the IRS tax website and consult with a CPA as your individual circumstances may not align with these general ideas.**

Mortgage & Rent

For your mortgage or rent you are able to deduct the portion of your space that is used for business as a home office, but this space cannot be used for anything else .[30] The deduction should be equivalent to the percentage of space for your home office or business operation based on the square footage. For example, if you have a 400 sqft office, used exclusively for business purposes, in a 1200 sqft home, then you can deduct approximately 33% of your total yearly mortgage or rent payments as a business expense. Again, the key here is that the space needs to be used exclusively for business. If you have a space in your house that is not being used for anything else, use it as your business office, storage facility,

[30] "Home Office Deduction" Internal Revenue Service. 27 September 2016.irs.gov/businesses/small-businesses-self-employed/home-office-deduction. 30 December 2016.

or for any other exclusive business related purpose. You will be able to deduct the same percentage of utilities (such as water, light and gas) that is proportional to percentage of the home being used for the business.

The requirement that the space be used exclusively for business and nothing else makes it difficult to use a significant amount of your home for business. One strategy that aligns with our social media strategy of making your moments a business and get one hundred percent of your home qualified as a business expense would be to make a movie about your life and use your living space as the stage. You will need to film every moment of your time in your living space. This will ensure it is being used for business and nothing else, as the filming is the business operation. You can then claim the living space as a set or filming location for content centered around your unique everyday life in your home. What you choose to do with the content collected from the filming is up to you. As the director and producer you can make the decision around what parts of the film to edit out. You can take the raw footage and package it anyway you like. You can release 5 minute clips summarizing your days or full 24 hour days. You can make a really long movie if you choose. The key is to publish something even if it is just 4 hours of that total recorded content.

This sounds ridiculous but in the age of people live streaming their everyday life it might not be. I could see the frenzy over 4000 to 8000 hours of someone's life available for viewing online. Beyond the amount of people interested, I can imagine the amount of time that will be spent watching one thing. A project like this could make significant ad revenue.

Personally I am too private to do this and the amount of filming would intense. Not to mention you would need to notify everyone that comes to your home that they are being filmed if you want to publish anything with that person in it. This strategy can be a bit extreme, but lucrative both in tax deductions and content creation. With the average rent and utilities being about $1000 and $150 a month respectively you are looking at $13,800 of business expenses that can be deducted against your taxes just for recording your life for a year.[31]

---

[31] The average rent and utilities depend on the size of the apartment or home. "Cost of Living in United States" Numbeo. numbeo.com/cost-of-living/country_result.jsp?country=United+States Accessed 19 October 2016.

Auto loans/leases

Auto loans are probably the second biggest expense for most people. With that said, if you have a auto loan or lease there is no reason you should not providing some type of transportation service like driving for Uber or Lyft. The deductions for automobiles used for business are a little particular and give you a valuable choice to make. You can take the standard mileage deduction, at the time of this book being written is 54 cents per mile ,[32] or you can figure out how many miles you drive for business vs personal and use that percentage of business use to deduct a portion of all your auto expenses such as repair, tag, title, gas, and maintenance.[33] It might sound like the second option is more advantageous, but taking the standard mileage rate typically works out to provide more business expenses. With the second option, your personal use is working against your business use. What I mean by this is with option two the more you drive for

---

[32] The standard mileage rate changes annually and is published by the IRS. "Transportation" Internal Revenue Service. irs.gov/publications/p463/ch04.html#en_US_2015_publink100033935 Accessed 19 October 2016.

[33] "Topic 510 - Business Use of Car" Internal Revenue Service. irs.gov/taxtopics/tc510.html. Accessed 19 October 2016.

personal use, the smaller the percentage of business use becomes. So if you find yourself wanting or having to make a multiple state drive you will hurt your tax deduction coverage for your car. With the standard mileage rate deduction it is straightforward. If you drive 5000 miles for business you will have $2700 in deductible expense, assuming 54 cents per mile, no matter how much personal driving you do.

Remember that Uber and Lyft only track the mileage you drive while transporting passengers, but does not capture the amount of miles you drive when waiting for a ping.[34] For example, make sure to keep a log of your own miles in the event you decide to drive to a surge area.[35] Although you aren't transporting someone, the miles you drive to get to the surge areas are still part of your business operation.

The good thing with either option is you can deduct improvements to the vehicle and regular cleaning

---

[34] A ping is a notification from the ridesharing service of a potential passengers request for transport.

[35] A surge area is a location that has a lot of ride request activity which causes the cost of the ride and therefore payment to the driver to increase.

services, so long as the cleaning or improvements are directly related to the business use of the vehicle. This provides a great opportunity for anyone looking to make aesthetic or functional improvements to your car. I'm sure there is some limit on how far you can take the improvements, but remember it is subjective. As long as you can explain how it contributes to your reviews, which keep you eligible to drive for these ride sharing services, then the improvements should be deductible.

If you are looking to get a new car the section 179 deduction of the tax code can provide you with a large bonus depreciation expense in the first year of ownership. Section 179 allows you to depreciate up to 80% of the cost of the vehicle in the first year. The vehicle must be used at least 50% for business. Multiply the percentage of use for business by the cost of the vehicle to get your first year deduction. This means if you have a vehicle that costs $50k and 70% of the mileage is used for some type of transportation or moving business (such as Uber, Lyft, or Dolly) then you can deduct $35k in the first year that you can use to payoff the loan. Sounds great but there are some additional exceptions to consider. Vehicles under 6000 lbs such as your standard sedan is capped up to $11,160 for a new car and $3,160 for a used car. For SUVs between 6000 lbs and 14,000 lbs used to carry passengers the limit is $25,000. The limit, however, does not apply to vehicles that seat 9 behind the driver's seat or equipped with cargo area 6 feet or more.[36]

Long story short, you have options of getting your new or used car paid for. My suggestion is if you are paying a lease, or considering buying a new car, add Uber or Lyft as part of your business operations. Drive to a nearby city that might offer higher rates such as New York from Philly. Those miles driving to the other city will give you lots of miles that can add up to tens of thousands of dollars. In just a couple years you may be able to pay off your car loan with your deductions.

Cell phone, internet and television.

Your cell phone, internet and television bills come in third as the most common expenses for Americans. Getting a full deduction on any of these are particularly hard because they are tied into your everyday life. For

---

[36] Section 179 has many exceptions that change the amount you can deduct. “Electing the Section 179 Deduction” Internal Revenue Service. irs.gov/publications/p946/ch02.html. Accessed 20 December 2016.

your home internet and cable television using the first idea of creating a movie from your life at home for a year would give you a 100% deduction because the use of these services is part of your life that you are trying to capture for your media product.

Alternatively, for the television services and subscriptions, if your business involved watching television, such as reviewing television shows and publishing your reviews online, then the television service would be deductible. The percentage of the cable or satellite tv used for your business of being a tv journalist will be deductible.

Internet is more difficult to get 100% deduction from and you will only be able to deduct the percentage that is used by the home office. Other than that you could produce media content around your experience using your internet provider for an entire year.

Finally, your smartphone is probably the hardest item to get a 100% deduction for because it is not tied to the home office as a passive cost. You can only deduct the percentage of your smartphone cost that is equivalent to the percentage used for business, which can be extremely difficult to figure out because of how often we use our smart phones without thinking. Most people solve this problem by getting a phone for the strict purpose of using it for business. However, the purchase of the phone and the service are two different cost items. If you need to purchase a particular type of phone to do something related to your business you can deduct that purchase, however, the service that you pay for monthly is not deductible for that reason. If your business involves consistent travel for example and you require a phone during your travel then your smartphone expenses are deductible during your travel time. It will be vital for you to maintain a record or log of some kind clearly distinguishing your business use from your personal use.

food

Food is an interesting monthly expense because it is variable depending on how, where and how much you eat. For some people dining out can be their most expensive monthly expense. Often unintentionally. But if you have an online food magazine or blog, that you are pursuing as a business, which focuses on a meals that you cook and eat, then those groceries and meals required for the production of your content would be a deductible business expense. Strangely enough many people have Instagram accounts made up of nothing but all of the meals they cook and eat; this provides Instagram content and ad revenue, but no profit for the content creator. With a simple picture blog, all of these meals or the contents of the dinner that you made from your groceries are a tax deductible business expense. The key is tracking in detail what is being purchased to produce the meals being showcased. If you are attempting to showcase everything that you make, then everything you purchase to make those meals are a business expenses.

travel

Travel can have a huge impact on expanding business opportunities and producing profits. Many people don't take vacations because of the expense, or save for months to take a vacation. Well, stop taking vacations and start taking business trips. If you are required to travel to a location because you need something to produce or promote a product then it is a business trip. Even if your product is travel articles. Everything that you experience that makes it into your writing is a valid business expense. There are many businesses that rely on work done or products produced in another country. While it is easy to develop these business relationships online to start a profitable business, face to face conversations are far more efficient. The efficiency gains from face to face communication or seeing a business operation in person allows you to justify your travel as a business expense. For anyone who has ever traveled on a business trip for a large corporation you should have an understanding of how this works. Your company sends you on a trip to have a series meetings. Sometimes you are forced to have after work dinners, but on those really enjoyable trips, your afternoons and weekends are your own, just like any other vacation. The difference with the business trips for your own business is that you have the freedom decide how and when you work.

Some non standard expenses such as subscriptions to Tidal or Spotify may qualify as a business expense. Companies often offer their employees subscriptions like this to allow them to avoid commercials that may be distracting if they are writing code or other works that require concentration. If a big company can deduct this expense, so can you.

The general theme here of reaching Maximum Tax Deductible Coverage is put in a little effort and turn your life into a business. Your social media life is already a business for someone else. Your presence, thoughts, pictures, etc are no less a product than an episode of Keeping up with the Kardashians. Sure it may be a nuisance and project may not generate a lot of income, but you have the potential to generate so vitally needed investment income for yourself and your community.

Audits

The most important part of achieving Maximum Tax Deductible Coverage, other than generating the business operations that result in expenses, is tracking your expenses. I take a picture of every business related receipt in a Google Keep note and add the label "taxes". As a backup I also have my credit card statement that I can use if I need to provide records of my expenses for IRS auditing. I also use Quickbooks to link my Shopify store and credit cards so I can ensure all income and expenses are accounted for and itemized. You should not be afraid of an IRS audit. In fact, you should operate under the assumption that you will be audited and be prepared for it with your records and receipts along with explanations for all your expenses. Remember that the evaluation of your business and its operations are subjective as to whether they fit within the legal guidelines that qualify for deductions. Chances are if you make enough income from your business will be audited eventually. The rule is, If you don't have a record of the expense then it does not exist. For that reason I also avoid paying for things in cash unless a receipt is provided.

Education and training

After you leave the structure of high school you have some difficult decisions to make about where you go for additional education. Many people, like myself, will elect to go to college. After college, you can seek an advanced degree to put yourself in a place to earn a salary that will afford the lifestyle you desire. The cost of this is typically paid for with loans you cannot free yourself from with bankruptcy, regardless the intention of the leader, thanks to the 2005 Bankruptcy Abuse Prevention and Consumer Protection Act.[37] Your student loans will follow you til death, unless you can prove undue hardship.

---

37 *See,* 2005 Bankruptcy Abuse Prevention and Consumer Protection Act. https://www.gpo.gov/fdsys/pkg/PLAW-109publ8/html/PLAW-109publ8.htm Accessed 18 November 2016.

Could you imagine any company taking on a loan that they could not discharge with bankruptcy? Perhaps if school was evaluated more like a business we would come to some different choices. The average college student will receive $30,100 in student loan debt.[38] This will result in paying $300 to $500 a month depending on how your repayment is structured. Longer repayment plans will result in paying up to two times the original loan through interest. What does a student get for all of this? The average college graduate earns $50,651 as of 2015.[39] If you think of your employment as a product being sold for $50,651, and the student loan is the cost of that product then you are looking at a 60% cost of the good being sold. In isolation this one time cost seems potentially reasonable because you are making a 40% profit margin. But in order to provide the service of your employment you have additional annual costs not ac-

---

38 The project on student debt provides state by state statistics on the student debt crisis. "Project on Student Data, State by State Data" The Institute for College Access & Success. ticas.org/posd/map-state-data. Accessed 20 November 2016.

39 "Average Starting Salary for Class of 2015 Climbs 5.2 Percent" National Association of Colleges and Employers. Fall 2015. naceweb.org/s11182015/starting-salary-class-2015.aspx Accessed 20 November 2016.

counted. Most importantly is taxes, which removes 25% of your income. You then have housing of about $12,000 a year using our $1000 a month average from earlier. You will need to eat, entertain yourself so you don't burn out. Probably most importantly is the daily or monthly compound interest of the student loans. Given all of this expense, it seems as though it will take many years before you break even. There has to be a better way.

Taking on this loan does not afford you the opportunity to deduct the expenses as a business could. Faced with the multitude of options for providing education to their employees without the benefit of deducting the expenses, a business simply would not make this kind of investment. So the question is, why would you? As a business, any related education necessary to run the business may be an allowed deduction because education and training is critical to business growth and thus related to generating the precious profit our government relies on.

Before we talk about options that can be deducted, let's talk about the particular difficulty in deducting undergraduate tuition as a business expense. The strategies that we are discussing in this book start from the perspective of someone who is working and paying taxes. This presents us with a problem for undergraduates, as many undergraduates are not working or making significant amounts of money to make a deduction worth while. The bigger issue with undergraduate education is that it is too general. Education has to be specific and related to a business to qualify as an business education expense.[40] You typically take many liberal arts classes that would be unrelated to your business. It would be almost impossible to tie these classes to a specific business operation.

Bootcamps, graduate school programs, and basically any other specific education could be a deductible expense for your business. Take for example the growing popularity of dev bootcamps for people looking to gain additional skills or make a career change. Dev Bootcamps can cost anywhere from $10,000 to $18,000 dollars.[41] That is one third to two thirds of the cost of col-

---

[40] "Tax Benefits for Education: Information Center" Internal Revenue Service. 15 April 2016. irs.gov/uac/tax-benefits-for-education-information-center. Accessed 20 December 2016.

[41] BLOC offers numerous developer bootcamps. You can find a full list on their site, bloc.io/coding-bootcamp-calculator.

lege. You should not make this type of investment as an individual; You should do so as a software development business. Investing in development education might seem like a waste of money when an offshore developer could be hired for much less than $10,000. But as the owner of your business you get to decide what type of expenses are best for your company. As I can attest from my own experience, knowledge of software development is an invaluable skill for a business or product manager.

Unlike undergrad, graduate school programs are extremely specific and tailored to getting you skills in a particular profession or industry. Possibly the most common graduate school degree is the MBA. The MBA was given so much praise for its wide application across different industries. This wide application, yet specific training and education, makes it a perfect education expense for any business. If you pursue an MBA, make sure you maintain the same corporation all the way through your program as the justification for the expense will get distorted if you start a program as an expense for one company and then continue the expense with another. Closing your initial business could create the argument that when the first business ended, your reason for the graduate program also ended and therefore you are not taking MBA classes for business reasons.

Don't Buy Anything You Can't Write Off (Stop Being a Spender)

The truly wealthy live a life far different than us. I am assuming that if you are reading this book you aren't already wealthy. The wealthy have millions and billions of dollars that could last across many generations. However, given enough time and a lack of knowledge on how to properly manage it, all that wealth could disappear within one generation. Managing money, in my opinion, really just means figuring out how **not** to spend it. In modern society, where basic necessities are typically dependent on the work of others, spending money is inevitable.

Growing up poor and black in South Florida many of the people around me had a propensity to spend their money on unnecessary luxury instead of more affordable alternatives. We shouldn't seek to condemn these purchases, just as we don't criticize the purchase of yachts, classic cars, jets and lavish apartments by the wealthy. Don't get me wrong, i'm not saying there isn't a problem with spending in the black community, especially amongst those with lower income. In fact, using Facebook's Audience Insight,[42] and filtering on interests particular to black people will show you that black people spend far more than your average Facebook user. I believe the thing that sets the average non-wealthy black consumer's purchases apart from many wealthy consumers' purchases is that wealthy consumers do a better job incorporating their spending into their business; thereby making their purchase a business operating expense or investment. We should seek to convert our spending into valid business expenses as well.

As I mentioned before, someone is profiting from your time, especially your time spent online. Whatever it is that you like to spend your time and money doing, incorporate it into your business operations. If you proclaim yourself a foodie, pop up a blog with paid advertising such as Google Adsense, and start owning your reviews and make those meals a business expense. If you are the outdoorsy type and find yourself driving distances

---

[42] "Audience Insights" is a powerful Facebook tool that can be used to learn more about particular target markets. You can find out more at facebook.com/business/news/audience-insights.

to take on new hikes, popup a blog with paid advertising or creating hiking maps for sale, and claim your mileage deductions, equipment, food and other expenses as operational expenses for your business. You don't have to create the next Facebook to take financial advantage of your life.

Creating a valid business expense is a mindset. Think of the IRS as your parents. Your parents set rules for you, but if you are a very effective rebel child then you recognize all the grey areas where you aren't quite breaking the rules. To transition your spending into valid business expenses you will need to be the rare rebel child, ready with an explanation for each expense, in the event you are questioned by your parental tax enforcers.

Chapter 4

The long term view

Now that you are a business and know how to turn your spending into tax deductions, your decision making just got a lot more complicated. Although we have spent much time learning how to get money back from net operating losses through pass through taxation, the goal is still to make a profit. That profit may not come immediately, which is why our gracious government allows us these tax concessions. In order to make decisions that lead to profitability and community rehabilitation, we need to first understand the long term view.

The long term view is not focused on the stupid question "think about your life in the next five years..." The long term view is not just about you at all. The long term view focuses on our community. The long term view looks ahead a generation or two.[43] If you have this view you are an empire builder. You are the person that can look at all the resources that surround you and plot a

---

[43] A generation for the purposes of this book is 35 to 40 years.

clear path. Your plans don't just include building something, but also maintaining it for the next generation to build upon. The long term view favors ownership, financial structures, and organizations within our community. The long term view will guide us to financial revolution and restoration.

There are three key components to the long term view. Understanding the effect of "compounding over time". Being able to spot where real money is. And understanding the value of assets over cash.

Compounding over time

One thing that is certain is the population will continue to increase. That is unless some massive disaster kills billions of people instantly. This truth drives much of the commodity values across the world. Your house increases in value because there is more demand for properties in your neighborhood. Basic supply and demand: the increased value is a result of fewer houses being available for sale, due to an increase in population in your area. The almost guaranteed increase in population means that if you buy a commodity and hold it long enough, eventually there will be a population to demand it. Assuming the commodity hasn't become completely useless to our society (Imagine a world where energy could be created from nothing, oil could become almost worthless). If you are able to remain in business long enough, the ever expanding population will provide your business with increased notoriety, exponentially spreading to more people assuming you provide quality service or products to your customers.

The ability to remain in business is determined by your grit and unwavering resolve. This probably applies to so many things in life, but in business especially you have to push through adversity. Many people do not see the adversity faced by successful people and companies and only pay attention to their success. Vice Media, came very close to failing before becoming an incredible media company success worth more than $4 billion .[44] In a span of 22 years Vice Media secured major investments

---

44 Listen even if its cable ratings are horrible" Nathan McAlone. Business Insider. 6 September 2016. http://www.businessinsider.com/why-vice-is-worth-billions-2016-9 Accessed 15 November 2016.to the founder of Vice Media, Suroosh Alvi, discuss their many near failures on NPR's "How I Built This" 10 October 2016. http://www.npr.org/podcasts/510313/how-i-built-this. Accessed 15 November 2016. "How Vice convinces the world it's worth billions -

twice and went broke twice. It took over a decade for Vice Media's content to be demanded by the mainstream as the world began to embrace the culture of their initially small underground market. The thing to note about the Vice's story is not just the success, but all the value and knowledge they built up from years of operation even though they were near failure. It may take multiple generations for your small business to find the right audience or strategy to have breakthrough success. By passing along the value and knowledge of your business to future generations, they have a chance of realizing the true value of what you've created. The very existence of your business will propel knowledge and resources to the future generations of the black community.

Real Money is where no one wants to be ... right now.

The great economic battle is supply versus demand. In my college economics courses we were taught that when there is a demand for something supply is created by the market to meet the demand. But if you build it, will they not come? The answer is generally no, however, things can get complicated when we take the long term view. Supply is built to satisfy anticipated or existing demand. The problem is, if you see the demand, so does many others. In real estate, if there is demand in a particular neighborhood and not enough housing to satisfy the demand, someone will build more housing. For example builders may buy existing space, to build something bigger, at a high price, that reflects the demand. The developer/ builder will then have to account for that cost in the sale or rent of their new apartments to make the venture worth it. You don't want to be the developer. The goal is to be the landowner selling to the developer after years of appreciated value.

Fortunes are built from purchasing or starting early. If you own something long enough, it is very likely someone is eventually going to want to buy it. Pointless trading cards become collectors items. Old Nintendo NES games are selling for thousands of dollars at hundreds of times more than their original $40 or $50 dollar price tag.[45] The property in gentrified neighborhoods sell for hundreds of times more than their original value.

Three years ago my wife and I purchased a condo in an area in Chicago called Logan Square, about 4 blocks away from the gorgeous, if infamous, Humboldt Park. North Logan has been an area for artist and non conformist for a long time, but the majority of the neighborhood, especially as you go further south, is primarily a Puerto Rican and Latino ,working class, neighborhood. This neighborhood has wonderful family structures and an unbelievably welcoming and supportive community.

Yet our favorite part of our neighborhood, Humboldt Park, was once notoriously violent, well-known for for gang activity, stabbings , shootings, and crime. It was not a place you could safely visit once the sun went down. But, wisely, we did not allow the recent history of Humboldt Park deter us from the potential for profit from investing in Logan Square.

South Logan Square is one neighborhood away from Wicker Park, a neighborhood stuffed with coffee

---

45 "10 Very Rare (and Very Expensive) Video Games" Rob Lammie. Mental Floss. 16 March 2016. mentalfloss.com/article/66183/10-very-rare-and-very-expensive-video-games. Accessed 20 November 2016.

shops, chain hipster boutiques, donut shops and overpriced ramen. Balancing the good and the risky, we bought our condo and have been able to see great returns.

Admittedly, we bought at probably the perfect time to experience rapid value appreciation. The city was in the initial phases of building a walking path, the 606 or Bloomingdale Trail, that cut through numerous neighborhoods in Chicago one block away from our condo. Within three years the neighborhood has some of the best restaurants in the city and has become one of the premiere nightlife locations. We paid a little above 100k and already the value has gone up fifty percent.   if this trend continues we could end up making one hundred percent profit when we sell the property. By buying when few others wanted to, we have made an investment that was almost guaranteed to have long term, exponential, returns. The point is that you should maximize your return on investments by choosing assets based on their potential for long term returns; not that appearance of immediate profitability. If you buy land in a "run down" neighborhood and hold it for 100 years, it's almost guaranteed that the land will be significantly more value then than when you bought it.

Typically a flashy well publicized investment that is being advertised to you is not something you want to buy or own. Think about how many people have come across the investment before you. The money spent on promotion is being factored into the price. If everyone is dying to get into a particular area you probably should not live there if you are looking to maximize your investment return. Just like you wouldn't want to create a business if there are hundreds of people doing the same business right next to you. I believe this is an important concept to grasp when trying to acquire wealth and financial growth within the black community because many assets in black neighborhoods perfectly priced to be purchased and accumulate wealth.

I believe our communities are sitting on valuable financial assets within our neighborhoods. The undervalued structures can be converted into businesses and residential rehabs to spark a black gentrification movement. As we start to revitalize our own neighborhoods with productive black owned businesses, the property value in these neighborhoods will increase. Overtime, as the demand for real estate in these neighborhoods increase, the value of these properties will also increase. We can then choose to sell our real estate assets instead of being priced out of our own communities as a result of gentrification.

You Want Assets not Cash

Paper currency aka cash is not worth the paper it is printed on or the pixels used to generate the numbers that display in your bank account. You might ask yourself, isn't the point of getting rich to get lots of cash? Well, no. Paper currency in the United States is backed by nothing .[46] Money is created digitally or printed at the will of the Federal Reserve System, a collection of banks authorized to create money on behalf of the United States. You should be focused on obtaining assets with real, tangible value; not paper with abstract value determined by human lead organizations.

---

[46] *See*, "Is U.S. currency still backed by gold?" Board of Governors of the Federal Reserve System. 2 August 2013. https://www.federalreserve.gov/faqs/currency_12770.htm. Accessed 21 November 2016. Money not backed by a commodity is called fiat currency. "Fiat Money" Investopedia. investopedia.com/terms/f/fiat-money.asp?lgl=no-infinite Retrieved Accessed 21 November 2016.

Paper Currency is an asset that is only given value because people believe it is valuable. When economies collapse or inflation rages out of control, the value of paper currency drops. If the US economy failed today all the money in your bank account would probably be close to worthless. Every moment you hold onto your paper currency in a bank account or in your hand it becomes less valuable due to inflation. This means if milk costs five dollars today, then in six months that same amount of milk could cost five dollars and fifty cents and maybe six dollars in another 6 months. So if you had five dollars today, in the future you would no longer be able to afford to buy milk with that money. That is the ravenous power of the ever hungry inflation monster. The reason behind why inflation is almost guaranteed to perpetually increase is a subject covered by many authors, but for the purposes of this book we will hold inflation as a constant truth. Inflation is the reason why many people use their paper cash to purchase investments in financial assets such as stocks in hopes to make a return that at least matches the rate of inflation.

While financial investments are better than just holding onto your "paper" currency, they are still inherently flawed from a long term view perspective. These assets are based on financial markets that are basically depending on cash to make cash. So if the underlying cash fails as mentioned before, you are still essentially left with nothing. The only benefit you would have is claiming your losses as an expense to reduce the amount of taxes you owe today and probably for years to come.

So now that I have said all that about cash, I'll give it one complement. Sort of like finding that one good quality in someone that you don't particularly like. Cash, in my opinion, is the best means for buying assets. If you have cash on hand you can often buy things for less, either because you avoid fees associated with loans, or you save procedural time associated with loans. Take for example the housing market in Atlanta Georgia in 2012, four years after the start of "The Great Recession" where housing values fell for the first time in decades and acquiring loans to purchase homes became extremely difficult.[47] Many people looking to sell their homes could only sell their homes for much less than their purchase price. However, these people still owed the banks the

---

[47] "The Great Recession" Economic Policy Institute. stateofworkingamerica.org/great-recession/. Accessed 28 January 2016.

original value of their loans, which in some cases was more than the market value of the house. So when these unfortunate home owners sold their homes, they would need to pay the banks the remainder of the loan even though they did not make enough in the sale for this repayment. Because so many people owed more than the value of their homes, many banks decided to cut their losses instead of going into expensive foreclosure proceedings and potentially getting nothing in the end because the homeowner could simply file bankruptcy. Sure bankruptcy would ruin the homeowner's credit but they would be excused from the loan they owed the bank. Banks instead agreed to short sales,[48] which freed the borrower from further payment obligation if their homes were sold for less than the loan amount owed. As a result, anyone that had enough cash could make a deal with the bank to pay much less than the asking price for the short sale because it cost the banks time and money to go through the short sale process. I attempted to purchases many homes that year, whether it be a foreclosure or a short sale, but every time the house would sell for much

---

48 "Real Estate Short Sale" Investopedia. investopedia.com/terms/r/real-estate-short-sale.asp Accessed 21 November 2016.

less than what I was going to pay with my bank loan. That would have been a great time to have a lot of cash on hand.

In the long term view, holding cash will adversely affect your financial growth efforts personally and for your community. You want to own assets whose sole value is not based in cash. Land, timber, rare coins or collectables, paintings, and even businesses are all good examples of assets that have a value outside of their cash value.

Now when it comes to owning parts of a business, you don't want to own stock in a public company long term, you want to own part of a business where you know the people running the business. Where you understand how it operates. My personal belief is that publicly traded companies are inflated in value for the short term and that you will not get the "real money" as we talked about in the previous section. If you took one thousand dollars and purchased twenty shares in Google at its lowest price, shortly after it went public, on September 4th 2004, ($50 a share) then you would have gotten twenty shares. You would have gotten twenty additional shares after the 2012 stock split, leaving you with forty total shares in Google today. So that initial thousand dollar investment would be worth $32,560 as of September 23rd 2016. So in just thirteen years you've multiplied your money 32 times. And for what we consider the long term view let's say that doubles or triples over the next twenty-five years, giving it a full generation of being publicly traded. You now have $97,680. Not bad.

If you took that same one thousand dollars and invested in a small local business, your potential for returns are exorbitantly higher. We'll ignore the risks of the business failing as we ignored the risk of the stock price going down overtime. For the sake of argument, let's say you invested one thousand dollars in a business "XYZ", worth $50,000 today for two percent of the business. In twelve years, the same time span Google has been publicly traded, XYZ is making one million dollars in profit per year. This is nowhere near the profits Google pulls in, but you are entitled to two percent. You will be making $20,000 a year from the XYZ profits if you choose to take your profits in cash. We'll ignore the value of XYZ because that is a complicated equation with many factors that we won't add to this example and we want to focus on maintaining ownership and the business value only matters at the time of sale. If profits for XYZ remained steady over an additional twenty-five years you would make $500,000. That is more than five times what you would have made investing in Google. Not to mention that XYZ would probably benefit from compounding over time and typically have increasing profits the longer they stay in business.

Cash does not serve our long term view. Nor do publicly traded assets designed for easy access. The long term view is not about liquidity (cash available for use) or participation in values determined by cash driven markets, such as the stock market. The long term view is about real growth across generations of people, businesses and communities. The long term view is planting the seed of a slow growing tree and knowing that it may not bear substantial fruit in your lifetime, but future generations will receive the fruits of your labor.

Chapter 5

How our new black businesses should work together

I want to now shift the focus away from you as an individual and focusing on our systematic approach to revolting. It's my hope that you are reading this book not just because you are concerned with how to get money to invest in yourself, but also how to take that money and play a role in the black economic revolution. Much of this is simply my theories meant to inspire greater minds than my own.

Stop Competing

Our entire lives we have been taught by a meritocratic society that we need to compete and rise to the top to be successful. We play sports and attend school where only the top students are recognized and are given the resources to succeed. This support builds exceptional individuals while the remainder of the group is left behind. In our black community, we are often objectively measured by the exceptional individuals, who become bearers of culture and possibility, that perhaps may never come because of this competitive structure. Wars are not won by exceptional individuals but by exceptional groups of individuals. After all, some of the most successful businesses have other businesses as their investors or their clients, which creates a symbiotic relationship.

When it comes to our new black businesses, we must look at one another as our support group, and provide each other the resources that will allow us to become an exceptional group and not just exception individuals. I recently listened to Margaret Heffernan's May 2015 TED talk titled "Forget The Pecking Order atWork" .[49] In part of her talk she discusses an experiment done with chickens, where the chickens who produced the most eggs were segregated from the other chickens for six generations and observed. When sepa-

---

[49] "Forget the pecking order at work" Margaret Heffernan. TED Conferences, LLC. May 2015. https://www.ted.com/talks/margaret_heffernan_why_it_s_time_to_forget_the_pecking_order_at_work Accessed 21 November 2016.

rated the normal chickens continued to be very healthy, plentiful, and continued producing eggs at a normal rate. However, despite an initial surge in production, after several generations the high producing "Super Chickens" had only a few chickens left alive because they had all killed each other.

The symbolism of this experiment's results should be obvious for the black community. The most talented and in some cases lucky are plucked from our communities to enjoy success in isolation. Yet this isolation from the community often removes intangible community norms critical for survival. While isolated from the community these successful black people may initially thrive but, after generations in isolation, their children and their children's children could lose their connection to the black community. In isolation future generations are assimilated into white culture and like the Super Chickens, and the culture which sustains them dies.

Promote Ownership for Strong Roots

Think of your business as a single tree and your eventual employees as branches. While the branches serve an important purpose, it is the roots that connect the tree to the forest of trees. It's been proven that trees in near proximity share and shift resources to help other trees survive when faced with threats.[50] This root system ensures that the forest will always survive and grow when faced with harsh conditions. The people you decide to partner with are your roots.

As a business owner you must remember that your company is part of a bigger movement for your community. When you are faced with bringing in talent to help your business grow, try to cultivate that talent. Instead of providing an employment contract consider amounts of equity or contracting this talent as an independent contractor to allow them the same opportunity to deduct expenses and grow their business. As the businesses you interact with grow, you will begin to create the root system that will share resources. These roots will stretch towards more diverse business opportunities. You want to avoid turning our community into employees. Hold them accountable for making themselves a business. We need

---

[50] "From Tree to Shining Tree" Radiolab. WNYC Radio. 30 July 2016. .http://www.radiolab.org/story/from-tree-to-shining-tree/ Accessed 22 November 2016.

businesses so we might achieve the full investment power required to lift our community.

The power of removing the employee structure within our businesses and promoting ownership is simple and powerful. If you are the owner of a restaurant for example, you will require at minimum, a chef and/or cook and a server. Typically these employees are paid hourly and given a basic employment contract to work as an at-will employee. These employees will be required to commute to work and have other expenses related to their employment which they will not be able deduct. As the only business involved in the work, only you can deduct expenses, if you decide to cover them that is. However, if you acquire the services of your cook and server under 1099 employment, your cook and server are now independent contractors; because of this hiring arrangement, two very important things happen. The first is you are able to deduct the cost of your cook and server's services as business expenses. The second is your cook and server are now independent businesses and have the right to deduct any expenses they think are required in running their business. This means their travel to work, any equipment they purchase, shoes, clothing, and most importantly education expenses may be tax deductible. The true underlined potential for your business filing the 1099 is the level of personal investment that your cook and server can make in themselves, which in turn becomes an investment in your business without you needing to be solely responsible for their personal development.

Partner as much as possible to build those symbiotic relationships. This might be more difficult from an operational standpoint in the short term. However, in the long term, spreading that money to multiple parties when possible increases the velocity which the money flows throughout the community.

Beyond the spread of finances throughout the black community, which will eventually serve to make you and your future generations' lives more financially stable in the long run, partnering when possible also helps to grow the social capital of the black community. Social capital is a term used to describe the efficiency of diverse groups.[51] One of the attributors to social capital is the diversity of ideas and problem solving with people

---

[51] "Social Capital" Investopedia. http://www.investopedia.-com/terms/s/socialcapital.asp Accessed 21 November 2016.

who view an issues differently. The capacity of people within a group, with different views, to solve problems together, may return more money to a partnership than one would have gotten by yourself. The compounding effect of social capital, if our community participates in this methodology of business practice, is an entire community that understands how our businesses work. This knowledge distributes the economic power of the community making it extremely resistant to the systematic attacks we experience today.

Cooperative Organization

So, let's assume you effectively operate a business around your lifestyle that enables you to recoup 50% to 100% of your income tax at the end of the year. What now? If you make the average $40,000 a year, then you now have $5,000 to $10,000 cash to reinvest in your business. But what to invest in? After all, in the grand scheme of operating a business or investing, $10,000 is not a significant amount of money. In addition to overcoming the insignificance of the individual income tax return, there is the harsh reality that not every black person that starts a business will have the ability or desire to run a successful business on their own.

Cooperative businesses or organizations are a unique type of partnership with a powerful potential to transform our black communities and black society across the world. Cooperatives are businesses or organizations created and operated explicitly to serve the needs of those using the services. Profits that are earned are distributed amongst the members of the cooperative.

Much of the power of cooperatives come from their democratic inclusivity, giving one vote per member. This is in drastic contrast to typical for profit organizations that provides voting rights based on the number of shares owned. Cooperatives have the power to democratize membership in an organization, which increases participation, leading to a democratization of skill and knowledge throughout the community. There are five types of cooperatives but we will only focus on the combinations of three, worker, consumer, and producer. A worker cooperative is owned by employees who are members.[52] A consumer cooperative is owned by consumers of the goods or services.[53] Producer cooperatives are owned by the producers of a type of commodity to bring structure and efficiencies to their industry.[54] Through the combined use of these three cooperative organizational structures, I believe we can provide black communities with healthy food options, better financial institutions, and alleviate a wide range of other social issues.

Healthy food options

Food deserts are geographic regions where access to affordable healthy foods are such as fresh vegetables does not exist within a reasonable traveling distance .[55] The issue of food within the black community is an issue we must take control of. In the United States access to high quality food that won't kill you over the long

---

[52]"Five Types of Cooperatives" Independent Welding Distributors Cooperative. http://www.iwdc.coop/why-a-coop/five-types-of-cooperatives-1. Accessed 20 December 2016.

[53] Ibid.

[54]Ibid.

[55] "Food Deserts" Food Empowerment Project. http://www.foodispower.org/food-deserts/. Accessed 24 December 2016.

term due to artificial fillers, genetic modifications or the addition of processed sugar should be a human right. The cost of high quality fresh produce that can be found in stores like Whole Foods is tying our physical well-being to our economic vitality. This link needs to be broken. With our combined investment cash we can partner together in worker/consumer grocery store cooperatives to provide healthy grocery store options. We should also establish producer cooperative farms to supply our grocery store with produce.

The producer farming cooperative should be established to ensure space and resources are being used efficiently to meet demands of the various grocery stores. Farming is a risky business. Many crops are dependent on particular seasonal weather conditions and thus the fate of many farmers can change with the weather. A cooperative can help share knowledge as well as the risk of farming. The cooperative should enforce standards across the various farms to ensure quality and reliability.

Our worker/consumer grocery stores will provide affordable, healthy food options for members at discounted prices. The discount should be established at the cost of acquiring the produce in addition to covering the operational expenses of the grocery store. The cost of employees should not be factored into operational cost because the employees will be the members of the coop, who are not paid for their service. Instead the deep discount of produce should serve as payment for work. Minimum working requirements should be established for membership, for example working at least 8 hours a week. A tiered discount system should be established to allow those with more time to benefit from their increased contributions. The goal is to find a balance for membership so individuals can contribute without impacting their other employment or business obligations, while still allowing those with more time to benefit from their larger time contributions.

Over time our grocery stores will bring in customers other than the original worker/consumers. Some of these patrons can be converted to members adding to the participation and strength of the cooperative. For those who do not become members, their patronage will add to the profits of the grocery store that will be distributed to the members. The recruitment of new members of the cooperative should be extended to anyone that shops at the grocery store and has the ability to meet the minimum work schedule requirements.

Management of our cooperative grocery store should be run as true democracy where each member has an equal vote regardless of the amount of financial contribution to the cooperative. While this democratic structure is core to the cooperative experience and enforces involvement of each member, businesses still need unique roles to function efficiently. Everyone at the grocery store cannot be a cashier. Who would stock the shelves? Your cooperative can either elect certain members for permanent roles such as general manager, or rotate members in various roles. I prefer the later because it exposes each member to the various parts of the operation, therefore spreading the knowledge evenly amongst your cooperative.

Better financial institutions and aid

There is a well documented history of discrimination against our community in the banking industry. Many of the practices that seemed to be a blatant practice of the past have persisted through more elegant and subtle means.[56] The impact of the discrimination from these financial institutions has negatively affected the black economic agenda of financial advancement, stability, and self reliance.

Gentrification, or what I like to call reverse "white flight," [57] has resulted in white people moving into predominantly black and brown neighborhoods. As white people move in the demand for businesses, such as food, drinks and entertainment increases creating a tremendous amount of opportunity. Starting these businesses often require a loan from a bank. Without these loans, the black residents are often excluded from the rising economic opportunity. Therefore, the original inhabitants of the gentrifying neighborhoods are forced to sell their homes and relocate as property taxes increase.

Cooperatives in the form of credit unions have an opportunity to ensure that the black community is not

---

[56] "Redlining: Still a Thing" Emily Badger. 28 May 2015. https://www.washingtonpost.com/news/wonk/wp/2015/05/28/evidence-that-banks-still-deny-black-borrowers-just-as-they-did-50-years-ago/?utm_term=.c2aa55e73fd9. Accessed 24 December 2016.

[57] White flight describes periods of time where white families fled the inner cities for the suburbs as black families began to move into those neighborhoods.

excluded from the economic opportunities that are created during gentrification. Our credit unions should run independently serving the needs of a local neighborhood. However, the should also work cooperatively with other black credit unions, to provide financial backing when opportunity presents itself but more equity is needed to accomplish a particular goal. Creating this type of financial structure will require stewards of community trust, such as our churches, to band together and take responsibility for the financial infrastructure of the communities they serve. We'll talk more about the role of our churches later.

Thinking broadly, cooperatives could be used to resolve issues social, housing, or even educational issues in the our black community. An education cooperative, lead by a collective our advanced degree black engineering parents, could providing tutoring programs and math academies. Cooperatives could be introduced in housing programs that provide a path to ownership by a local credit union for member renters. The possibilities are numerous if not endless. I challenge you to conceptualize how cooperatives could be used to solve some of the issues we are facing. A great book to understand the history and applications of cooperative organizations is "Co-operative Courage: A History of African American Cooperative Economic Thought and Practice". We need to establish organizations that work not just for our people but are worked and owned by our people collectively to democratize operational knowledge of our communities. This will ensure that the fall of one or two black leaders does not equal the economic downfall of our black communities.

Chapter 6

The role of our churches

I am not a religious man personally, but I spent much of my youth in many forms of the Christian churches. The gothic chanting of Catholic services, Christian rock, and Baptist holy ghost dances all amused me. My fascination was for the people I saw to be the most devoted. The people most victimized and taken advantage of by our pyramidical society of greed in America. Despite growing up poor in south Florida, I did not feel as though strength from the church was realistic or needed. I had an internalized sense that I was better than my circumstances because of my pride in being Jamaican. I've always felt it was up to me to change my fate with my decisions. I feel the same way about our black community.

The places we turn to for strength cannot do the work that is needed to lift us all. Their arms are too short to reach the heights we need to go. It is our responsibility to partner with our churches as a user/owner cooperative to create community centers. I will be using the word church in this section to represent mosques, temples, ziggurats or whatever religious center black people might frequent.

Let the government pay your tithes and offerings

Before I get into the strategic role of the church I have to mention the importance of your tax deductible donations to the church, also known as tithes and offerings. One of the most frustrating things to me is watching people give their money to nonprofits without getting any tax benefit for themselves. If you are a devoted patron of your church, then chances are you give ten percent or more of your income to the church. These donations will not be counted on as business expense as part of your schedule C itemized deductions, but as part of your normal deductions. You will then have to make a choice between your standard deduction and itemizing your deductions, which would include the church donations. For 2016 the standard deductions are $6300 if you are filing individually, and $12,600 if you file jointly.[58] In most cases, the standard deduction will be higher, but at least provide yourself with the option in the event you make some other large donations that year. The cumulative deductions are what adds up to big returns.

For example, let's say you donated ten percent of your paycheck to a church and in that same year donated an old car valued at $5000. Using our $40,000 average salary, depending on your state taxes you would have donated roughly $2800 to your church. Your total donations would equal $7800 from your car and church donations, which is $1500 more than the standard $6,300 deduction. However, if you did not track the donations made to the church throughout the year you would be leaving $1500 on the table come tax season.

Connecting People

Churches serve one of the most important parts of this financial revolution. Our churches are one of the only places that we can go and be around members of all

---

[58]"2016 Federal Tax Rates, Personal Exemptions, and Standard Deductions" Internal Revenue Service. https://www.irs.com/articles/2016-federal-tax-rates-personal-exemptions-and-standard-deductions Accessed 26 November 2016.

social classes from the poor and homeless to celebrity athletes, musicians and wealthy businessmen. To the black community, even in communities with intense violence, the church is, as they say in Marvel's Luke Cage series, Switzerland. The church is sacred neutral ground where those who would never speak due to chance proximity or social beliefs have an opportunity to find common ground. This common ground is what we need to make this financial revolution work on a macro-scale.

During my time in Chicago I have attended Trinity United Church of Christ, the famed church of Rev. Dr. Otis Moss III and Pastor Emeritus Dr. Jeremiah Wright. In three years I have attended actual church service about four times, but I have gone to probably many church events. This is because Trinity does a great job of providing councils to handle specific issues in the black community such as social justice reform through their prison ministry, to which my father-in-law is devoted. They provide financial classes, couples counseling and other services to reinforce the stability of the black household. But faced with a global systematic attack on blackness, defense is not enough and one church can not be a shield to a frontal assault while we are surrounded.

A bond between religious groups within the black community is needed, not just for defense but to coordinate aggressive financial strikes. Within churches like Trinity United Church of Christ the congregation should be organized by location. Each of these locations should meet to discuss the needs in their neighborhoods along with a representative from the church. After the top priority is democratically agreed upon by the neighborhood representatives, a cooperative should be organized to help satisfy the need. In the case where a church happens to also own and operate a credit union, which is a cooperative, the representatives should work with the church as a whole to acquire the funds to invest in the creation of the cooperative. If a church does not have a credit union, then they should promote the collection funds for these special projects to start these cooperatives. The creation of these cooperative entities should not exist in the name of the church, rather the church should either be a member in the cooperative or the loaner of funds. This will ensure the people of the individually segmented neighborhoods take an active role in solving their own problems with the guidance and support of the church.

Supporting Our People

Our communities will require a sense of accomplishment to continue solving their own problems through cooperative organizations. This means our churches will need to educate themselves on the personal finances of the black community that they are responsible for. Churches should look to add accounting, tax advisement, and business consulting services.

Any great company knows that taxes are an active part of your business plan throughout the year and not just something that is handled at the end of year. Many churches offer tax services around tax season, but by this point it is impossible to apply a tax strategy that would provide the deductions needed to recoup most of the money being paid in taxes. Members need to have access to someone to investigate their life and spending habits and devise a business strategy around that spending. This method would provide the greatest deduction against income tax.

Many people are used to working as an employee and can find business ownership or 1099 contracts overwhelming. Admittedly as an independent contractor or business owner there is a greater responsibility because you must figure out how much taxes you have to pay at the end of the year instead of having it deducted from your paycheck. User/owner cooperatives will turn members into owners of a business which may result in profits or losses that each individual member will need to know how to handle.

Religious groups should have tax advisors who donate their time to help congregants control their financial lives year round. The subject of this advice should be around keeping businesses legal and expenses legitimate and trackable. Moreover, people should be able to consult advisors before making major purchases or commitments to consider the best course of action for incorporating the purchase into their business operations. By providing these services and staying connected to the economic success of individuals, the church will be ensuring the continued participation in and therefore success of our financial revolution.

Conclusion

Moving Forward

My hope for this book, with the most selfish of intentions, is that black and brown people invade the white fortresses built in the most prominent areas of cities all over the world. That I might one day visit a city and not notice where the white space ends and the black space begins.[59] If your desire is to experience the same, I invite you to share these words in hopes they spark the rebel spirits. I recognize all the answers won't be found in this book as it is targeted specifically at the US Tax Code, but hopefully it sparks minds to create systematic ways to fight our continued social and economic oppression.

---

59 White space vs. black space is a concept that certain areas are designated for white people and some are designated for black people. People are also presumed to carry the attributes of their space with them as they cross between these spaces. For an example of white space vs black space, see "Black vs. White Space in McKinney, TX" Sandra Bertin. 16 June 2015.
prindlepost.org/2015/06/black-vs-white-space-in-mckinney-tx/. Accessed 20 December 2016.

Often it seems things rooted in blackness are appropriated and only become financially viable when there are non-blacks do them. We call this appropriation, but from the standpoint of economics, when something is popular it will be controlled by those with money. This is why it is vitally important to keep things black-owned so we not only benefit financially, but can afford to maintain our cultural innovations. Ownership must be maintained in the face of lucrative offers to purchase property and companies. Internalize this single message, the real value and thus money comes with time that spans many generations.

In war drastic measures are taken when faced with an enemy seeking to eradicate your way of life. America faces enemies wishing to remove their influence over the cultures of the remainder of the world. The US has dropped atomic bombs, conducted experiments on soldiers, started wars in foreign nations, and destroyed foreign economies with sanctions. As great as the threat is to the United States, there is a bigger threat to black people in America. Much of the world's wealth is controlled, as you can see by looking at the top 100 richest people on

Forbes' list.[60] Blackness faces systematic genocide in the United States, [61] South America and even in Africa. In the face of this global systematic oppression and attempted assassination of black cultures, I offer a systematic approach to begin fighting back here at home in the United States. My proclamation for this book is that we as black people should lift each other up, not with the vague words of spiritual and religious guidance existing in duality as inspiration and blockade, but with coordinated action. I offer a general code of conduct and customs as a foundation to be built upon, so that generations to follow can reclaim their honored seats as the drivers and builders of humanity; that they may shed the burden of misguided disdain.

---

[60] "Forbes 400: The Full List Of The Richest People In America 2016
" Chase Peterson-Withorn Forbes 4 October 2016. http://www.forbes.com/sites/chasewithorn/2016/10/04/forbes-400-the-full-list-of-the-richest-people-in-america-2016/#5f8bdf1653b4. Accessed 26 January 2017

[61]"'We Charge Genocide': Systematic Murder & Oppression Of Blacks Continues In US" Kit O'Connell. Mint Press News. Kit O'-Connell. 11 August 2015. mintpressnews.com/we-charge-genocide-systematic-murder-oppression-of-blacks-continues-in-us/208539/ Accessed 26 December 2016.

Made in the USA
Monee, IL
08 November 2026

67380777R00065